DON'T PANIC

The Procrastinator's Guide to Writing an Effective Term Paper

(You know who you are)

STEVEN POSUSTA

BANDANNA BOOKS • SANTA BARBARA

Don't Panic: The Procrastinator's Guide to Writing
an Effective Term Paper (You Know Who You Are)
© 1996 Steven Posusta

Bandanna Books
319-B Anacapa Street
Santa Barbara CA 93101
Email: bandanna@west.net
800-259-8324

Quotations from *The Metamorphosis* by Franz Kafka,
translated by Professor Stanley Corngold,
Translation copyright © 1972 by Stanley Corngold.
Used by permission of Bantam Books, a division of
Bantam Doubleday Dell Publishing Group, Inc.

The text of this book is composed in Calisto, with
cover font Twylite Zone by Oliver Conte Design.
Text designed by Words Worth of Santa Barbara.
Cover design by Joan Blake.

First Edition
10 9 8 7 6 5 4 3 2

LC 96-84169
ISBN 0-942208-42-0

Visit our website for college self-help
http://www.west.net/~bandanna

CONTENTS

Procrastination is the thief of time.
—EDWARD YOUNG

PREFACE

The Academic System

Writing papers for college or university professors can be terrifying. The first paper I ever wrote came back to me flowing with red ink. A note on the first page read: "Why did you ignore my instructions? Rewrite!" I had unfortunately interpreted the professor's instructions as mere suggestions. Papers are personal, aren't they? If I answer the question and speak my mind, I'll do fine, right? Wrong.

Several college and English writing classes later, I began to understand that academic writing is a specialized system with its own unique rules and practices. The more rules I learned, the more my papers improved. Later I became a successful English major and a composition tutor. I have since tutored hundreds of students—both undergraduate and graduate   in their writing.

During these tutoring sessions, I began to repeat myself with startling frequency, and, I discovered that most students write just like I do: at the last minute. The vast majority of students wanted speedy methods to solve the same recurring problems. As a result I developed ways to quickly steer struggling writers in the right direction, unleash their creativity, and show them the keys to revision.

To my dismay, I found that no writing manual sufficiently demystified the writing process. Even the smallest books on composition are over 100 pages in length. These books will not help you if your paper is due in a week, let alone two days. If you're pulling an all-nighter you'd be completely on your own. This book changes all that.

The Quickest Way

Few students even form organized plans for writing their papers, let alone follow them. This, by itself, gives you a tremendous advantage. The particular method I have presented in this volume remains the quickest complete method that I have encountered and personally practiced.

This does not mean, however, that following my "simple" method removes the need to work. It remains impossible to write a paper without first reading the assigned material and, most importantly, thinking about it. Someone completely ignorant of the classroom material will never be able to form a thesis, no matter how "instant."

But if you have done your reading and thinking, the procedures set out in this volume can serve you well time and time again. Simply follow the procedures in this book, and they will become instinctive. I have attempted to clarify the composition process, clearing a pathway for you. You only need follow the path to fluent, confident, and rapid writing.

How to Use This Book

Don't Panic is divided into two sections: THE ROUGH DRAFT and REVISING THE ROUGH DRAFT. If you have not started writing your paper and have no draft to work with, use this book from beginning to end. First we define your topic with an instant thesis, then do a freewrite, and you'll have a rough draft in a hurry. The next step involves the introduction, conclusion, and easy fixes for major errors. If you are desperate or masochistic, it is possible to complete both steps in one all-day or all-night session. This kind of procrastination pressure often results in inferior work, undue stress, and premature hair loss. I don't recommend it, especially for your first attempt.

If you already have a rough draft written, you should read about the *Instant Thesis* in SECTION ONE, and then skip to SECTION TWO. The instant thesis will help you locate and focus the thesis you already have before moving on to the revision section. You should be able to complete this in one evening, even during your first experience with this book.

Most techniques in this book take longer to read than to practice. Your first attempt at this method will most likely be your slowest. I would suggest a two-day time schedule for the first paper. After you master the process, you will probably work much faster and use the book only for an occasional reference.

The sample starting on page 57 shows how an actual A paper looks. Your finished paper should have a similar appearance, with clean type, evenly spaced paragraphs, an introduction, a conclusion, and proper quotations. The sample exists for you to see how all the things mentioned in this book mesh together in a finished paper. But don't even think about copying the sample and turning it in as your own. Somebody in your class might have the same idea. Besides, there is a subliminal message in the text that says *"I am plagiarizing, please fail me."*

I would like to thank my mother, Kathi, for teaching me everything I know, and my father, Stan, for sending me to school to learn more. Thanks also to Cheryl Giuliano at the UCLA writing program for all her time and valuable instruction. A final thanks to Joan and Sasha for having faith.

1: THE ROUGH DRAFT

Getting Serious

I submit the following statement: *the fastest way to write a paper is with word processor or computer.* Word processors and computer word processing programs make writing papers extraordinarily easy. If you are still banging away on an ancient typewriter or (dare I say it) writing with a pen and paper, you are at a serious disadvantage. A goose-quill pen may be oh-so-romantic, but nothing compares with the convenience, built-in editing tools and *speed* of word processors.

If you bought this book you are probably serious about your grades, and students serious about their grades need access to a computer. This book contains word-search methods that are ideally suited to computer applications. For example, a computer can scan ten pages of text for the word "from" in about two seconds. Searches by eyeball are another story. If you do not have a computer, try using one at a campus lab. If it's too late for that, you'll have to make do the old-fashioned way. Use a computer next time, though. Students using computers are writing their pages faster and neater than you are. You want more motivation? They sit next to you in class.

If you are like most students, your paper is due embarrassingly soon, and you have no clue what to write. You believe that your classmates are fearless, smarter than you are, more disciplined, and already finished. You're wrong. Nine out of ten people are just like you, waiting until the last possible moment to get started. I'll tell you a secret: you are probably starting earlier than many others. Don't panic, everything will be fine.

Your paper will develop in two phases. First, you will create a rough draft in a hurry. Then, in the second phase, you will revise your rough draft and fix everything that is wrong with it. If you already have a rough draft, skip to SECTION 2: REVISING THE ROUGH DRAFT.

The Instant Thesis

"My professors said something about a thesis."

They certainly did. A thesis is nothing less than your paper's main idea. If your paper doesn't have a thesis, it doesn't say anything. If your paper doesn't say anything, it will have missed the point. If you miss the point, your professor will give the A to someone else. Never fear. I will save you with my formula for an *instant thesis*. It works for any paper or essay on any subject.

Thesis helpers come in many forms. I first encountered a fill-in-the-blank thesis in a college handbook, but they are rather common. Many professors show similar devices to their students to help them discover their theses. I simply made this one fast and easy to use. Now burn the following formula into your memory:

#1. Although _____,
(*general statement, opposite opinion*)
#2. nevertheless _____.
(*thesis, your idea*)
#3 because _____.
(*examples, evidence, #1, #2, #3, etc.*)

By simply filling in the sentence's blanks, you can make a thesis about anything. As proof, I will formulate a nearly impossible thesis. Let's say something really outrageous, such as "Albert Einstein was an idiot." If we just fill in the three blanks, it will work.

Start with your idea, whatever you want to prove. We'll write our idea in blank #2: "Albert Einstein was an idiot." Then, to fill in the top blank, we need to write a general statement about Albert Einstein, or the exact opposite of the thesis in blank #2. A general statement would read something like: "Most people thought Albert Einstein was a genius." Fine. The last blank is a little more tricky. Write your reasons and evidence in blank #3. I just happen to know silly things about Albert Einstein. For example he never learned to tie shoelaces, and as a child people thought him dim-witted. Let's fill in the blanks:

#1. Although many people thought Albert Einstein was a Genius,

#2. nevertheless he was an Idiot,

#3. because he never learned to tie his shoelaces.

Presto! An instant thesis! It doesn't sound half bad either, even though we offer weak evidence. No one would refute Einstein's genius for lack of a simple skill, but this proves that no matter what your ideas are, you can use the "instant thesis" to clarify them. Once you have a thesis to write about, you will not waste your time.

Take some time right now (if you have it) and practice writing a few theses. They can be about anything. Just get used to the format, and you'll be cranking them out faster than you ever imagined. Here are a few samples (both serious and silly) to help give you the feel:

#1. Although <u>many people think the earth is round</u>,

#2. nevertheless <u>it is actually flat</u>,

#3. because <u>my Uncle Sven sailed off the edge</u>.

#1. Although <u>Shakespeare was a great dramatist</u>,

#2. nevertheless <u>his play "The Winter's Tale" is flawed</u>,

#3. because <u>it attempts to combine comedy and tragedy in one work</u>.

Finding the Hidden Thesis

"What's the easiest way to find a thesis?"

Most professors love to give paper topics that I call "freshman nightmares." Freshman nightmares are paragraph-long paper topics that seem too convoluted to determine what the professor wants. Students struggle at length with these assignments, only to misinterpret them and then write confusing, unfocused essays. I will show you how to use these complicated instructions to your advantage, and find a quick thesis that is right on the mark.

Milk the question to find the hidden thesis. By "milking" I mean searching the assignment to find what the professor wants. If we read between the lines, these questions do our work for us. This may seem strange, but more often than not, your professor will practically give you a thesis, and save you the trouble of thinking one up. We only need to recognize what she or he has given us.

Lengthy assignments are truly a student's best friend: they yield the most information. This makes it extraordinarily easy to get a thesis quickly, and the faster you get your thesis, the faster you start writing. Here is a complex assignment that we'll milk for a fast, easy thesis:

> Plato argues that politics require the city to create members with just souls. According to Plato, how is justice in the city the same as justice in the individual? What is his argument? Does he convince you? Discuss.

Wow. The assignment, though brief, packs a wallop. Three questions wrapped in one, followed by the unnerving and ominous word "discuss." Truly a question fit for nightmares. Luckily we can fill in the blanks in the instant thesis and solve this problem fast.

LOOK FOR CONTRAST

The most important blanks in the instant thesis are the first two. Notice that the first statement contrasts the second one. The secret to a good thesis is *contrast*. You must show how your main idea (thesis) differs from the obvious or common opinion. To make a bold thesis (and you must be bold), search the professor's question for places where contrast exists. Milk it for drama and conflict. The above example contains three questions:

> 1. How is justice in the city the same as justice in the individual?
> 2. What is Plato's argument?
> 3. Does he convince you?

Question #1 doesn't seem to contain much contrast. The definition of justice sounds complicated, and is probably something best saved for the paper's body.

Question #2 is more general than question one. It

refers to Plato's argumentative technique. This question may have a place in the paper, but probably not as your thesis. It's hard to say something contrasting about what Plato's argument is.

Question #3 is the only one left, and luckily it just what we need. Does he convince you? The answer to that can be very bold indeed, either a bold "Yes" or a bold "No." The key element is *contrast*. Obviously this professor wants the students' opinions about the class reading. The professor wants you to take a stand, and argue that Plato is right or wrong. This sets up a simple "yes" and "no" conflict to fill in the first two blanks in the instant thesis:

> #1. Although <u>Plato argues with great conviction about justice</u>,
> #2. nevertheless <u>his argument does not convince me</u>
> #3. because _____.

(Of course you could just as easily write a thesis exactly opposite: *#1. Although Plato discussed justice over two thousand years ago, #2. nevertheless his arguments are still convincing, #3. because....*)

YOUR TURN

Okay, time for the thesis for *your* class assignment. No time like the present to start chipping away at that nasty procrastination. This part's easy, so go ahead and take a few minutes now to fill in the first two blanks with your own thesis, making sure there's a contradiction.

#1. Although _____

_____

_____

_____,

#2. nevertheless _____

_____

_____

_____,

#3. because _____ (*evidence will go here*) _____.

Now all that remains is to fill in your evidence for whichever thesis you choose, using the instructions from the PROVING THE THESIS section. If you have completed the instant thesis, move on to that section now.

One more word about the thesis: it is not written in stone. You paper's subject can change if you want to change it, but whatever thesis you end up with, stick to it! If your thesis reads, "This play is awful," you had better not talk about how much you liked Act Three. Be consistent! Formulate a bold thesis and prove it, even if you decide to prove Einstein was a dolt and Plato was a fool. Readers may disagree, but at least your point will be clear and well made. Everyone will know what you are saying, most importantly you and your professor.

Compare and Contrast

"Wait! I'm suppose to write a compare-and-contrast paper!"

Professors often assign the dreaded compare/contrast essay. Usually the professor presents two or more works for the student to either compare or contrast to each other. The essay assignment usually reads like this:

This quarter we have studied the religious and ethical teachings attributed to Jesus Christ, Buddha, Lao-Tze, and others. Choose two prominent figures and write an essay in which you compare and/or contrast their views on righteousness, divine and earthly love, sin, and the human condition.

"Hey, that's not fair!" you scream into your roommate's ear. "How am I supposed to do that?"

Not only are you being asked to compare *and* contrast, you have to deal with two subjects instead of one! Your professor is a fiend!

Hold on, things are not so bad. Remember the first thing to look for when forming your thesis is *contrast*. How quickly we forget. Albert Einstein was a genius, *but* he could never tie his shoes, or Plato lived long ago, *but* his ideas still apply. This kind of contradiction is built into the compare/contrast essay. You don't even need to make up your own thesis, because your professor gives you one. In the above assignment, the only thing for you to decide is whether Jesus and Buddha are alike or different. Simply write the answer to that question in thesis blank #2:

> #2. nevertheless <u>Jesus and Buddha teach similar ideas</u>,

or:

> #2. nevertheless <u>Jesus' teachings contradict Buddha's</u>,

We know that blank #1 needs only to contradict #2. Notice that when we flesh out the above examples, we have two distinctly different theses:

FIRST INSTANT THESIS

#1. Although <u>Jesus and Buddha represent different religions</u>,

#2. nevertheless <u>their teachings are often similar</u>,

#3. because <u>(reasons and evidence go here)</u>.

SECOND THESIS

#1. Although <u>Jesus' teachings sometimes match Buddha's</u>,

#2. nevertheless <u>there is an inherent difference in their views</u>,

#3. because <u>(reasons and evidence go here)</u>.

The important thing to learn here is that in any compare/contrast essay you really have only two choices. Agree or disagree. Alike or different. Yes or no. Convincing or unconvincing. There is a duality built into the question, making it easy to choose sides. All that remains are the reasons *why* you chose your thesis. I will explain proof in the next section, but remember, whatever thesis you choose, you must stick to it!

MAKE A CHOICE

Now we need to find the contrast or contradiction in your assignment, fill in both sets of blanks below, stating the thesis one way (although similar, they are different) and then the opposite way (although different, they are similar). Then take a few minutes and figure out which argument you would like to argue.

19

Your First Instant Thesis

#1. Although _____'s ideas are
similar to those of _____,

#2. nevertheless _____ conflicts
with _____,

#3. because ____*(reasons and evidence goes here)*____.

Your Second Thesis

#1. Although _____'s ideas are
different from those of _____,

#2. nevertheless _____ is
similar to _____,

#3. because ____*(reasons and evidence goes here)*____.

Compare and Contrast Structure

Structure also presents a problem in compare/contrast assignments. Students often write difficult and unorganized essays while attempting to canvass two works simultaneously. There are two simple approaches to a paper involving multiple authors.

The Two-Segment Approach

The first and perhaps simplest option involves writing the paper in two distinct segments. Following a thesis that introduces both authors, you write a complete and independent essay on only one author in question. Then, with the first author out of the way, you are free to compare or contrast the second author with the first. This

20

method serves well when you understand one author or topic better than the other. You can display your extensive knowledge in the first portion of the essay, leaving the other for the second portion. The compare/contrast analysis that comes in the second half then serves to camouflage any shortcomings concerning the second author or work. A useful trick indeed!

A six-page paper matching this description could be diagrammed like this:

> [Instant thesis paragraph introducing Jesus and Buddha]
>
> [Pages #1 through #3 discussing Jesus, followed by]
>
> [Pages #4 through #6 discussing Buddha, followed by]
>
> [Conclusion which mentions both Jesus and Buddha]

ALTERNATING PARAGRAPHS

A second structural option involves alternating between the two authors throughout the paper. One paragraph about Jesus would lead to one on Buddha, leading to Jesus again. This method works well when you want to contrast several different points. It may be desirable to offer Jesus' views immediately if Buddha's teachings are complex and numerous. The reader may not remember Buddha's opinion by the time Jesus' contrasting view appears at the paper's end. A diagram for this method would appear like this:

> [Instant thesis paragraph introducing Jesus and Buddha]
>
> [Page #1 discussing Jesus, followed by]

21

[Page #2 discussing Buddha, followed by]
[Page #3 discussing Jesus, followed by]
[Page #4 discussing Buddha, followed by]
[Page #5 discussing Jesus, followed by]
[Page #6 discussing Buddha, followed by]
[Concluding paragraph summing up Jesus and Buddha]

Choosing the method most suited to your subject serves two purposes. First, merely having a plan sets you apart from many other students. Those who blunder through the assignment with no plan of attack cannot produce a quality product. Merely following a plan will automatically prevent many errors that commonly occur in student writing. Second, your chosen method will accent your material and ability to the greatest advantage.

Now that we have discussed the particulars of compare/ contrast essays, we only need to flesh out our thesis with solid evidence. In the compare/contrast essay, remember to think of your argument in terms of duality. For every piece of evidence, you must argue in terms of two authors or works instead of one. Find areas of common ground or conflict between your two authors or works, and there you will discover the best evidence to prove your thesis.

Proving the Thesis

In order to strongly argue a thesis, you need strong evidence. The third blank in the instant thesis forces you to succinctly summarize your supporting pieces of evidence. Often the evidence you have will dictate which thesis you attempt to prove. If you have more evidence that Jesus and Buddha differ, that may be the thesis to choose. If you choose to argue the opposite but have no proof, you may need to do more research before you start writing. The choice is always up to you. It often helps to number all the major details you can come up with, and list them as part of your instant thesis.

SHAKESPEAREAN THESIS

Although <u>the characters in Shakespeare's Othello uphold their public images</u>,

nevertheless <u>their private passions determine their fates</u>,

because:

#1. <u>Iago's desire to corrupt others leads to his death</u>,

#2. <u>Cassio's pride leads to his dishonor and death</u>,

#3. <u>Othello's jealousy destroys his wife and himself</u>.

STUDENTEAN THESIS

Although _____ *(general statement)* _____ ,

nevertheless _____ *(your thesis)* _____ ,

because:

#1. _____

_____ ,

#2. _____

_____ ,

#3. _____

_____ .

23

Depending on the length of your paper, you may need more topics for evidence. Three ideas are usually sufficient, especially when one contains a large issue that can yield many pages. For example, it may take several paragraphs of writing involving text quotations to discuss Othello, the play's main character. The actual number of evidence topics can vary, and only you can judge whether you have enough to meet the professor's page requirement. If you can only come up with one or two, try to narrow your topics. Maybe your one solitary evidence topic actually contains two or three smaller sections. As long as you have enough with which to start writing, go on to the next step. We can always add or delete ideas later.

The Optional Objection

If your assignment calls for a longer essay, or you have become familiar with this book's basis method, you may wish to add an "objection" to your instant thesis. An objection is nothing more than an imaginary disagreement that someone could have with your thesis. In the process of arguing your thesis, somewhere in the middle of your paper, a sentence like this would appear: "... of course it is true that (blank) is the case, but ...." This sentence introduces an idea contrary to your thesis, which you then proceed to disprove, or prove irrelevant to the discussion at hand. When you introduce and disprove a contrary point, your paper is more complex.

In a way, the "objection" appears as another manifestation of blank #1 of the instant thesis. It merely presents another "opposite opinion" for you to refute. If you were to add an objection to our Shakespeare example, it could appear like this:

Although the characters in Shakespeare's *Othello* uphold their public images,

nevertheless, their private passions determine their fates,

because:

#1 Iago's desire to corrupt others leads to his death,

#2 Cassio's pride leads to his dishonor and death,

#3 Othello's jealousy destroys his wife and himself.

Objection: It is true that Desdemona's public image and private self are identical,

But her subordinate position as Othello's wife links her fate with his.

STUDENTEAN THESIS WITH OBJECTION

Although _____ *(general statement)* _____,

nevertheless _____ *(your thesis)* _____,

because:

#1. _____ *(hot reason #1)* _____,

#2. _____ *(reason #2)* _____,

#3. _____ *(reason #3)* _____.

Objection: It is true that _____

_____

_____,

But _____

_____

_____.

25

You may place your objection anywhere you like in the paper's body. Often, the content of the objection will decide that for you. In the above example, Desdemona would be discussed along with her husband, Othello. The complexity that the objection brings to your paper can make the difference between a good paper and a great one. Once you have the basic method down, you should begin experimenting with this worthy technique.

Freewriting

"I have a thesis. Now what?"

Now that you have completed the instant thesis, you need to brainstorm, or as we whimsical writers say, *freewrite*. Freewriting is just what it sounds like—writing with total abandon, paying no attention to grammar, punctuation, paragraphs, or even writing complete sentences. To freewrite properly, you must only have the paper's length and thesis in mind. Your professor decides the length—that's done for you. And, if you've "milked the question," as I discussed earlier, much of your thesis also came from the professor. You can rest easy knowing that your professors are the source of so much information. We are on the right track to giving them what they want. Now we just have to fill in some more blanks. Add an additional blank to the end of each "evidence" blank in the instant thesis. We now have three more blanks to fill:

> #1. Iago's desire to corrupt others leads to his death _____
> _____(*etc.*).
> #2. Cassio's pride lead to his dishonor and death _____
> _____(*etc.*).

26

#3. Othello's jealousy destroys his wife and
himself _____
_____(*etc.*).

For each of the above blanks, you will freewrite as much as possible, for as long as possible, with as much detail as possible. Start with the first statement and write everything you can think of that falls under the heading of Iago. Include every idea, scrap of argument, write down key words, quotations, and other pieces of evidence that you have floating around in your head. Write it all in one big, flowing, stream-of-consciousness paragraph. The idea is to get everything in your brain onto paper. When you have exhausted the possibilities for blank #1, move on to #2 and repeat the process, and then on to #3.

I have found freewriting very effective when divided in this way. You can relax and let the words flow, while remaining on the topic. When you have exhausted idea #1, idea #2 remains untouched, a fertile ground for another freewriting session. Obviously this method alleviates boredom (which is why we hate papers to begin with), and is much simpler and more effective than attempting to freewrite an entire paper start to finish. Think of it as a road map or blueprint to guide your creativity, which prevents you from getting off track.

Let It Flow

"How do I get started?"

Do not stop if you misspelled something, mistyped something, or can't remember a quotation accurately. Let nothing interrupt your train of thought as it rambles down its track. Our objective is to create a rough draft right now. It is *supposed* to be messy. We will rewrite and polish later, so for now grammar and punctuation do not exist.

If you are a chronic perfectionist who can't let a single unpolished sentence slip by, a computer or word processor can help. Merely turn off or dim your monitor so you cannot see what you are writing. This trick also helps alleviate writer's block. Hide the type, and you can better concentrate on your thoughts. Of course, when pulling an all-nighter most students do not have time for writer's block. An impending deadline somehow seems to miraculously cure this condition.

Intermittent stops and starts are common when free-writing. Our minds simply work that way. Often the brain-storm drizzles for a bit before the floodgates open. If you have a ten-minute lag while waiting for your next idea, just be patient, it will come. When you get bogged down, don't peek at the screen! I forbid you! Simply sit quietly (or jump up and down) and stare at the blank screen until the words flow again.

Another reason to type your work is that handwriting is comparatively slow. When your train of thought turns into a runaway locomotive, even fast typists cannot keep up with the words streaming out of their heads. This process may sound mysterious to you if you've never experienced it, but believe me, it happens! Relax and let your freewriting instincts loose, and the words will flow with amazing speed.

LENGTH

"How long should the freewrite be?"

How much freewriting you need depends on the length of your paper. For instance, if a professor assigns me a four- to six-page paper, I will brainstorm and freewrite until I have filled about four pages. If the assignment asks for five pages, freewrite four and a half. For a ten-page paper, write no more than nine pages. Always freewrite a little less than what the assignment calls for. This may seem odd, but you

28

don't want to write more than you have to, do you? I didn't think so.

The length of your freewrite will increase later as you refine your work. You will add words here and there, polishing up your sentences and editing. You will also be adding an introduction and conclusion to the paper in Section Two. These additions more than compensate for the things that get deleted. Often five pages of freewriting will yield a six-page paper when all is said and done. So, if your freewrite is a tad short, don't worry, you are on the right track.

SAMPLE FREEWRITE

Here's a freewriting session using our Shakespeare thesis. Your freewrite should look like this one, with similar errors and typos that come from writing with abandon.

#1. Iago's desire to corrupt others leads to
his death—In Shakespeares play Othello, the
characters are 11 seemingly larger than life.
Thyey are all people whose minds are
sophisticaled, and seem in control, at least in
public The three main figures aro Othello,
Iago, nnd Cassio, three men whose posiirions in
the positical and milirary worldofvenice keeps
them in the public eye. Becauase they are all
thre concerned with their public images theyare
forced ot hide their true inner selves but
these inner truths cannot be denied no matter
how hard they tryand itis their inner selves
that eventually lead to their downfall. Iago is
a major character who puts on a facade for
others he is called "honest Iago," but he is
the most dishonest of peopleat heart. Iago
pretends to be the good companion and firend of
Cassio, but secretly wants to move up onto his
rank in the military. He also pretneds to be
Othelo's friend, but trries to destroy his
marraige and admits that "I hate the Moor."...

29

```
look up page. Iago's first acts that reveal his
inner character come in the first act where he
tries to stir up argumetns about othello's
marriage. His henchman, Brabantio, follows
Iago's orderes to cause disturbances in the
streets of venice . . .
```
(Continue freewrite until ready to move on to #2,
then on to #3.)

YOUR FREEWRITE

Okay, let's get started on *your* freewrite. I promise you relief
when you're done. Grab that cup of coffee or tea, get comfortable, dim or turn off your monitor, take two deep
breaths, and start writing. Just start filling in blank #1 in
one huge paragraph, writing whatever comes to your mind
on the subject, move on to #2 when you run out, then on to
#3 and you're done!

CONGRATULATIONS!

You have finished SECTION ONE. Look at your paper right
now. You have a working instant thesis followed by three
(or more) gigantic paragraphs of freewriting. It still looks
messy, but guess what? You are holding a rough draft in
your hands. This prize represents a hard day's work (or
less, I don't want to know). Now you can go to bed, go out
and party, or do whatever. Worry about the rest of it tomorrow. At least you are not pulling an all-nighter.

"Hey, wait! I am pulling an all-nighter!"

What? You mean this is due tomorrow? Don't panic; I'm
here to help. I created this manual for this exact situation.
You'll be fine, just a little worse for wear tomorrow. You
and I are going to finish SECTION TWO tonight and get that
paper in on time.

2: REVISING THE ROUGH DRAFT

Step One: The Body

If you are lucky, you've had a good night's sleep and we are ready to get back to work. The first thing we are going to tackle is your paper's body. You know, that big mash of mumbo jumbo that you spewed while freewriting. I know it looks scary, but we are going to fix it up. We will do an instant introduction and conclusion last, so don't worry about them yet.

As you look at your freewrite, you should see very large paragraphs—one for each idea in your paper. In our Shakespeare example we have three, but you may have more or less, depending on your assignment. So far your paper at least has some logic to it. You have three (or so) topics of evidence, all supporting your thesis, and all separated into their own very large paragraphs. Hey, that doesn't sound so bad, docs it? You've done more than you thought! Now we are going to jazz up what you have.

ELIMINATE OBVIOUS ERRORS

First, scan your work one line at a time, eliminating every *obvious* mistake. We will fix major errors later, for now just worry about the easy things. Check your quotations, names, or dates if you were guessing before. Change spellings, obvious typos, put in punctuation, and separate things into sentences as best you can. If you did freewrite with your computer monitor off, you will probably have many typos. Word processing helps a lot here. Any spell-checking or grammar program can clean up your paper in no time.

As you start to fix up your paragraphs and make sentences, you may need to type in extra words and sentences in order to make sense out of things. Do it! Type in as much extra as you want. Remember when I said your paper ends up longer than the freewrite? This is where it happens. Most of your thinking should already be on the page, and these extra phrases are just for clarity. Often this kind of editing can jar your thoughts, giving you lots of new sentences and ideas. Add them if they fit your thesis, but do not stray. It's too late to start all over again. Finish cleaning up idea #1 before you move on to #2. This will make it easier for you to focus.

PARAGRAPH BREAKS

After you finish editing your sentences, separate your three long paragraphs into separate, smaller paragraphs. Look for places where you changed gears within the large paragraph, and break things up there. Each paragraph should contain one major idea.

Most of your paragraphs should contain at least three sentences, and many will be longer. Long paragraphs are not uncommon, but page-long paragraphs are forbidden! There must be at least one paragraph break on every page. Further, if only one paragraph break exists on the page, place it in the *middle* of the page, if at all possible. Why? I'm sure you've seen textbook pages printed as a solid block of text with absolutely no breathing space. You hated it, didn't you? The text appeared boring and oppressive before you even started reading. In advertising, for example, ad writers surround text with as much empty space as possible. Years of market research prove that white space soothes the eye and accents the text. The reader approaches the message with an open mind. The last thing ad writers want is to turn off the customers *before* they read the ad! Your situation is identical. Include white space on every page, and sell your professors your ideas. Do not turn them off before they even start reading!

Have mercy on your professors and they will reward you with a good grade. Remember, they are reading every paper written in the class. How many students are in your class? Twenty? Thirty? More? Now imagine the professor grading yours last! This is yet another freshman nightmare, and a great reason to include a lot of paragraph breaks.

QUOTATIONS

Quotations do nothing more than give specific textual evidence to support your thesis. If a quotation isn't necessary, don't throw it into your paper for no reason. Conversely, don't forget to use a quotation when it is necessary to do so. Quotations are the best concrete evidence you have at your disposal. Writers err when they either quote too much, or too little. The trouble comes in finding the right balance.

A professor once told me to think about quotations as the chocolate chips in a cookie. If you ate a chocolate chip cookie, you would want lots of chocolate chips sprinkled evenly throughout the dough, wouldn't you? If there were no chocolate chips, you would be disappointed. Similarly, if there were one giant blob of chocolate in the cookie's center, you wouldn't want to eat it.

A paper functions the same way. If your paper has no quotations in it, you will have no evidence for your thesis. Your reader will go hungry. Further, you cannot make up for this lack by placing a huge paragraph of quotations somewhere inside your paper. This too will turn the reader's stomach. Sprinkle quotations throughout your paper and your reader will eat up your thesis.

Essentially there are two kinds of quotations: short and long.

Short quotations

Most students are comfortable using short quotations in their papers. You should easily incorporate them into your own sentences. Try to mesh the two, as in the following example:

```
The protagonist, lost in the woods, confronts
an old woman who "knows which way the wind
blows."
```

Sometimes it is easier to divide a quotation into two sections, with your explication in the middle:

```
"Watch the path," the old woman cautions her,
"or you will lose your way for certain."
```

There are infinite possibilities when it comes to formatting your quotations. Just keep your options open and take what your material provides.

Long quotations

Long quotations will not fit into a sentence, and must stand on their own. If you are quoting a passage that takes up more than four lines of your paper, you must separate it into its own paragraph. Simply indent ten spaces from your left margin, and indent the whole paragraph. You do not need quotation marks around a block quote, but you do need to place a blank line between your text and the quotation itself. Notice in the following example that the quotation is introduced with a colon, as long quotations often are:

. . . and we may discover this truth if we turn our attention to the novel's most important paragraph:

> I could barely fathom the depths of depravity to which I had sunk. All seemed lost. My soul yearned for some explanation, but there was none. No one heard my weak whimpering cries. No one felt my pain and shared it with me. I alone was a single, solitary, wretched being. I craved an end to my protracted misery.

This paragraph shows the depth of shame and self-loathing the protagonist feels. Many consider this situation to be directly . . .

As you can see, large quotations take up a lot of space, but if you try to use them as filler, your professors will catch on. Should you decide to use a long quotation in your paper, make sure that the entire text is necessary. Do not quote a whole paragraph if you only need one sentence to prove your point.

Step Two: Logical Sequence

Your paper's body is now segmented and somewhat grammatical. Time to examine the logic. We need background information before we can understand the details. That's why stories always move from general to specific. Take a reader's perspective. What would have to come first in order for you to understand? Often the general introductory material stands out clearly. Luckily, our instant thesis is designed to move from general to specific. This much is done for us.

Your freewriting should proceed step-by-step right along with the instant thesis. If your reasons and evidence were arranged logically to start with (and they probably were) your freewrite should also have an inherently logical structure. Look at your evidence blanks (p. 23) and consider the order.

In our Shakespeare example, a freewrite would begin with Iago, progress to Cassio, and conclude with Desdemona. This arrangement seems fine. Iago and Cassio are minor characters. We should probably discuss them first and leave the main characters, Othello and Desdemona, until the end of our paper. This seems a logical build-up of our material, but we could place Cassio first and Iago second. Or, since Iago dies last in the play, we could save him for last. The possibilities are endless. I only require that you have a reason for the order you choose.

Look at your rough draft and consider the order of things. Ask yourself questions. Does your thought progress smoothly? View each paragraph as a movable section, and examine the order. Do your paragraphs read logically? Do any of your paragraphs make more sense if you swap them? Try not to get too carried away with making changes. Often your first instincts about your material will be the best. If you cannot decide what to change, trust your original instincts and change nothing.

Step Three: The Instant Introduction

Now that we have an orderly body for your paper, we need to write an introduction—the "instant introduction." How fast is it? So fast, *we've already written it!* How, you ask? Remember our instant thesis? Now it will become our instant introduction.

An ideal opening paragraph always moves from the general to the specific, also. The first sentence always acts as a gradual introduction to the subject, and as the reader moves through, the paragraph becomes more detailed. This also, by design, is the structure found in the instant thesis.

Since you've already filled in the instant thesis, you are set up for a proper introductory paragraph. We only need rewrite the thesis sentence as a paragraph. Simply write a complete sentence for each blank in the instant thesis. We will turn our three-part sentence into a three-sentence paragraph—an introductory paragraph! Amazing, isn't it? Watch what happens to an instant thesis using *Frankenstein*:

FROM THESIS...

Although <u>Mary Shelley's *Frankenstein* is considered a gothic horror</u>,

nevertheless <u>it actually exposes Shelley's troubled family life</u>,

because:

#1. <u>There are no strong female characters or mothers</u>.

#2. <u>All family units in the novel are incomplete</u>.

#3. <u>The monster personifies an unwanted child</u>.

...TO PARAGRAPH

Mary Shelley's Frankenstein remains one of the most disturbing and horrifying gothic novels ever written. Perhaps the most disturbing aspect of the novel is its correlation to Mary Shelley's family life. Shelley's mother, who died in childbirth, is reflected in the novel's lack of strong female characters, or mothers. In fact, all family units presented in the novel are incomplete, and the monster itself personifies an unwanted, unloved child.

Wow, did we write that? It's amazing! We're amazing! That sounds like an A paper! And it all came out of our little thesis. It doesn't seem so "instant" when you read a paragraph like that, does it? Only we know how easy it was. Your professor never will.

Notice how the first two blanks of our instant thesis set up the situation nicely, leading the readers carefully and logically toward your pieces of evidence. By the time your readers get to the end of the instant introduction, you've already convinced them that you are on the right track. They *want* to believe you; they're ready to listen. If you make a small mistake later in the paper's body, you'll get the benefit of the doubt. Why? Because they trust you. Someone who writes a paragraph like that *knows what they're doing*. From now on, that's *you*. You have a plan of attack, and that makes all the difference.

Wrong Ways to Begin Your Introduction

Too simplistic

If you begin too generally, you will end up with something like this:

```
People have always been curious about solving
problems. Two people who thought about problems
were Plato and Aristotle.
```

The above introduction takes triteness to a new level, and sounds amateurish and shallow. Of course people have always been curious. You need a little more focus on the topic than that!

The "I'm not worthy" opener

```
I stared across the blank paper, wondering what
was required of me. An essay. A thesis. What
were these things? Well, I gave it my best shot
and . . .
```

Don't laugh. People actually do this. Why? I don't know. Never start a paper this way. It's too breezy, too self-absorbed, and you will sound like a teenage idiot.

The "too many questions" opener

Who was Mary Shelley? When did she live? Why did she write? What did she write? Who were her parents? How did she come up with the idea for Frankenstein? In this essay, I will answer some of these questions . . .

Questioning can effectively begin a paper, but only if you do it the right way (see pp. 40 and 42). The error usually lies in too many questions that are only loosely related. Do not get too general, too apologetic, or too wacky in your introduction. Stay specific, confident, and interesting. How? I thought you'd never ask.

RIGHT WAYS TO BEGIN YOUR INTRODUCTION

There are several techniques you can use to begin a paper that will grab the reader's attention. If you have trouble creating a sentence from your instant thesis, or just want to add spice to your beginning, try one of these:

A short quotation from an appropriate source

Mary Shelley wrote that she was often asked "how I, then a young girl, came to think of, and to dilate upon, so very hideous an idea." This hideous idea produced the novel Frankenstein.

A blunt, shocking statement

Frankenstein is the product of one young woman's deviant imagination.

A description of the paper's purpose

This essay will show how one young woman's family problems surfaced as a horrifying gothic novel.

How did a young woman of eighteen come to write one of the most horrifying novels in the English language? How could Mary Shelley's young imagination possibly produce the gruesome tale <u>Frankenstein</u>? As I will show in this essay . . .

YOUR WAY

Now that you understand how to create an interesting introduction, turn back to pages 17 and 23 to refer to your own instant thesis and evidence. Construct your introduction from your arguments, and place it at your paper's beginning. Now your term paper has a good beginning.

Step Four: Instant Conclusion

Now are you ready for something *really* easy? How about an instant conclusion? What is a conclusion but the exact opposite of an introduction? The introduction moves from general to specific, and the conclusion moves from specific to general. Just write your introductory paragraph in reverse! Watch:

FIRST REVERSE THE THESIS

(#3) <u>The monster personifies the unwanted child</u>.

(#2) <u>All family units in the novel are incomplete</u>,

because (#1) <u>There are no strong female characters or mothers</u>,

nevertheless <u>it actually exposes Shelley's troubled family life</u>

Although <u>Mary Shelley's *Frankenstein* is considered a gothic horror</u>,

40

Okay, now let's reverse yours:

(#3)_____

_____

_____.

(#2)_____

_____

_____,

because (#1) _____

_____

_____,

nevertheless _____

_____

Although _____

_____,

Now Write the Concluding Paragraph

In conclusion, Mary Shelley's monster mirrors
her own childhood suffering and guilt. Without
the family unit that is virtually non-existent
in the novel, and without a mother to love it,
the monster symbolizes Shelley's own childhood
feelings. Shelley's novel, then, is as much a
tale of dysfunctional and broken families as it
is a frightening horror novel.

Notice that both the instant introduction and instant
conclusion contain only three sentences. They will stand as
they are, but you may wish to embellish them a little more

41

for a personal touch. Any embellishment can only help to clarify and strengthen the foundation built on the instant thesis. Try these:

End with a quote

> "No father had watched my infant ways,"
> reflects Shelley's monster, "no mother had
> blessed me with smiles and caresses . . ." The
> unloved creature's absent family illuminates
> Shelley's lack of a mother . . .

If you began with a question, end with an answer

> How, then, did Mary Shelley's imagination
> produce **Frankenstein**? As I have discussed in
> this paper, Mary felt guilt over her role in
> her mother's death.

Use effective concluding words

Certain words and phrases can contribute to that intangible "concluding feel" that all good conclusions have. Use these phrases to construct your conclusion and you will be on the right track to a good conclusion:

"In conclusion ..."
"Finally, ..."
"Overall, ..."
"Consequently, ..."
"Above all, ..."
"In short, ..."

The above techniques can only help to clarify and strengthen the foundation built on the instant thesis. Paste your conclusion on the end of your paper. At last we have all our sections in place, not to mention two extra paragraphs. It is now time for STEP FIVE.

Step Five: Seek and Destroy

Your paper now has an introduction, a body, and a conclusion. That's all any paper needs. If you read your paper from start to finish, it should make sense. The first and last paragraphs are probably the best parts, with some good paragraphs and nice sentences in between. Rejoice, the end is in sight! But there remain those sentences and paragraphs that are not so good. What do we do about them? I am going to tell you a secret.

My secret, learned after many years of trial and error, is this: there are simply some words and phrases that you should avoid when writing papers. Why? Because if they show up, you've done something wrong. It may surprise you to learn that certain words pop up time after time in bad writing, and are almost non-existent in a well-written essay! Just eliminate these "bad" words, and any writing with improve dramatically. It's almost magical. Our next project is to "seek and destroy" these bad words. In doing so, we will destroy the writing errors they signal.

ERROR #1: PASSIVE VOICE

Even though I cannot know what you've written, I do know that the passive voice is likely to be your biggest problem. How do I know? Because passive voice is everybody's biggest problem. I've written a lot of papers, and even I can't get away from it completely. What is it? The *Harbrace College Handbook* defines it as: "The form of the verb which shows that its subject is not the agent performing the action to which the verb refers but rather receives that action: 'The ham *was sliced* by Emily.'" With definitions such as this, no wonder nobody knows what passive voice is, let alone how to fix it. I'll try to explain.

There are three main parts to a basic sentence: subject, verb, and object. In a sentence using the active voice, the

43

subject "does" something (whatever the verb is) to the object. But watch what happens when the subject isn't doing the doing—the *object* is. In the following sentence, the subject is Polonius and Hamlet is the object; but who does the stabbing?

Our Example:

<u>Polonius is stabbed by Hamlet</u>.
    S.   V.   O.

Textbook Example:

<u>The ham was sliced by Emily</u>.
    S.   V.   O.

Both of these are ineffective; they are examples of the passive voice. Notice that although they have the structure of a normal sentence (subject/verb/object), they really are topsy-turvy, with <u>victim subject/passive verb/actor object</u>. In a sentence written in the *active* voice, the *actor always comes first!* The correct sentence structure for academic writing is the active subject, then verb, then object. In order to fix passive voice, just exchange the subject and the object, and leave the verb in the middle (but change it to its active form):

Our Corrected Example:

<u>Hamlet stabs Polonius</u>.
    S.   V.   O.

Corrected Textbook Example:

<u>Emily sliced the ham</u>.
    S.   V.   O.

Presto! Passive becomes the active voice instantly.

"So what's so terrible about the passive voice?"

You are no doubt wondering why no one ever told you about the evils of the passive voice before. You should understand that there is nothing inherently wrong with the passive voice. It has many uses in fiction, and many textbooks frequently use it. You may discover that to express certain shades of meaning you have no choice but to write a passive sentence. We use passive speech on a daily basis. It isn't our fault that the active voice doesn't come naturally. Passive voice is, however, less direct and forceful than active voice. Also, it tends to collect prepositional phrases like a magnet. Long passive sentences containing many prepositions give your prose a monotonous and plodding tone. There is simply no room for this in academic writing. Some professors will stomach no more than a few passive sentences in an entire paper, and habitual use is forbidden.

Here's my secret

What? You want an easier way to fix the passive voice? You don't want to scan for subjects and objects in each and every sentence you write?

Well, okay, you've twisted my arm. The secret is in the examples above. Notice that the structure went from acted-upon/verb/agent to agent/verb/acted-upon. Now also notice that the verbs changed also. "Is stabbed by" and "was sliced by" became "stabs" and "sliced."

What is missing? Yes, you've got it! The "by" is missing! That one little word disrupted everything. That one, little, stinking word! How can it have such power? Because "by" is often an overused preposition. Overused prepositions are an extremely common error in student writing, and they nearly always signal passive sentences.

Spot the offending prepositions

Fortunately there are only a few repeat offenders that routinely destroy good writing. Here they are, in order of evilness:

1. **by**   (*Passive*) The answer was given *by* her.
   Better: She gave the answer.

2. **of**   (*Wordy and Passive*) The beginning *of* the
   story *of* the war was given by her.
   Better: She began the war story.

3. **from** (*Wordy and Passive*) A message of
   urgency came *from* her husband.
   Better: Her husband sent an urgent
   message.

4. **for** (*Wordy and Passive*) A cure *for* the disease of
   cancer may be found someday by doctors.
   Better: Doctors may someday cure cancer.

5. **to**   (*Passive*) A chew toy was given to the dog.
   Better: The dog received a chew toy.

These are the words you most need to "seek and destroy"—set your computer to scan for them, and eliminate as many as possible. It's that easy. When these words appear in groups, they signal a passive or otherwise awkward sentence.

Here are some examples of the way the words above can combine to create awkward, confusing sentences. The words to "seek and destroy" are in caps.

Incorrect:
Ellen came to be the head OF her own department.

Corrected:
Ellen heads her own department.

Incorrect:
From the very beginning OF the novel Jake is OF
the opinion that someone is stealing things
FROM his house.

Corrected:
As the novel opens, Jake suspects his home has
been burglarized.

Incorrect:
The Catholic priest tried to escape FROM the
people that he feels betrayed BY.

Corrected:
The Catholic priest, feeling betrayed, tried to
escape.

I should now say that you will not be able to remove all prepositions from your writing. They are often grammatically necessary. If you notice in two of the above examples, the word "to" remained in the sentences, even though we removed the other prepositions. The wordy expressions and passive constructions are gone, though, and that is what matters.

There are exceptions to every rule, and sometimes passive voice is necessary to retain a certain idea or phrase. That's okay. A few passive sentences are almost always present in any writing. Pages and pages of them will kill your paper and your G.P.A., but one or two are harmless.

If your word processor will calculate a percentage of passive voice sentences for you, aim for below 20% at first. Even this will probably be a tremendous improvement for you. When the active voice begins to come naturally, shoot for single-digit percentages. Seek and destroy!

ERROR #2: VAGUE VERBS

One of my professors told me that "at the very least, you should write verbs that crackle." That was good advice.

47

Verbs give all the action and energy to our sentences. Weak verbs make our sentences limp. Luckily, there is an evil verb for us to seek and destroy. It's called "to be" and it remains the worst verb in the English language. Unfortunately it *is* also the most common. (See? I used one of the forms of *to be* in this sentence!)

"To be" or not "to be"

Seek and destroy in your paper every form of that verb and replace each instance with action verbs; see the following list:

1. is
2. are
3. was
4. were
5. be
6. been
7. being

Why does the verb "be" create problems? It conveys the most meaningless state of existence: no motion, no action, no nothing. Something just "is" and that's all. Horrible! When you get rid of "be," the results speak for themselves:

Bad: The main character *is* speaking to a crowd.
Better: The main character speaks to a crowd.
Best: The main character preaches to a crowd.

Bad: She *is* fighting the enemy.
Better: She fights the enemy.
Best: She clashes with the enemy.

Bad: The trees *were* about to fall over.
Better: The trees appeared ready to fall.
Best: The trees threatened to fall.

When you replace weak "to be" verbs with verbs that crackle, your writing becomes intense and dramatic. Notice how the "better" sentences above improve when we simply remove the "to be" verb. Further notice how the drama increases when we replace a common verb such as "fight" with "clashes." More power, more color, more action, and more A papers!

ERROR #3: VAGUE PRONOUNS

In order to have strong sentences, we need strong verbs and nouns. Unfortunately people often use pronouns (he, she, it, etc.) where a noun would be more effective. Overused pronouns create confusion and the sense that the writer does not have a grasp of the topic. Look at the following example:

Incorrect:
`This is the kind of thing he was always doing.`

What is this person talking about? The writer should replace "this" and "thing" with the topic these words refer to.

Better:
`The main character cannot break his cycle of alcoholism.`

Now at least we have a topic for this sentence. Pronoun errors only occur when the writer doesn't use specific terms. In bad academic writing, vague pronouns usually appear with the "to be" verb. The two go hand in hand. When you locate overused pronouns in your paper, they will almost always be in combinations like these:

it is logical that ...
this is because ...

that is the reason ...

he has been ...

Avoid this type of "bad verb, bad noun" combinations at all cost. Since overused pronouns, weak verbs, and the passive voice go hand in hand, we are in luck. Our "seek and destroy" method will locate them that much easier. Usually when you discover a hidden "by" or "be," a sneaky pronoun in the sentence will also need fixing.

Watch for overused pronouns

Add the following pronouns to your seek and destroy search, and you'll have located and fixed most all your errors:

1. it
2. this
3. that
4. she/he

Remember, you won't be able to remove them all. These parts of speech are necessary for the English language. A few here and there are fine, even necessary. Write more than a few and you are in trouble.

Step Six: Instant Style

Now that your paper reads cleanly, flows in a logical sequence, with no more passive voice errors, crummy verbs, or vague pronouns, we can go for some quick style. Writing style comes with practice, but here are some tricks that most of us can put to good use.

STYLE TRICK #1: VARY SENTENCE LENGTH

The best writing sounds natural. Even though we are writing academic papers, they should not sound mechanical or robotic. Often students tell me that their papers, after eliminating the passive voice, sound stilted and repetitive. "All the sentences sound the same," they say. Sometimes they are right, but not because there is anything wrong with the active voice. Even if their sentences sound repetitive, they are still better than the passives they had written earlier. Their mistake lies in repetitive sentence length.

To cultivate natural, rhythmic sentences, you must vary their length. Your paper will sound abrupt and mechanical should you write too many short, declarative sentences. If all your sentences are three lines long with four commas each, the repetitive clauses will lull the reader to sleep. Break it up a little. Throw in a long sentence here, and a tiny sentence there. Like this. Get it?

STYLE TRICK #2: LINKING PARAGRAPHS

Now that your sentences flow, check your paragraphs. Can we read from one to the next without making any giant leaps of logic? If not, it may be time to throw in some linking words. This method is a "cheap" way to get your paragraphs to flow. Simply take a word from the last sentence of a paragraph, and use it early in the next paragraph. Check out this example:

> . . . are known as the "power elite," control everything. They are the upper-class, the corporate leaders, the think-tanks, and the policy-shaping organizations. Because these organizations have similar conservative views, they are in a position to dominate America's political climate.
> The power elite use their influence to . . ."

The repetition of the catch-phrase "power elite" will cause readers to connect the two paragraphs, and create an illusion of "flow" in their minds. Granted, your logic from paragraph to paragraph should flow without this trick, but sometimes it comes in very handy. Always try to repeat something from paragraph to paragraph.

STYLE TRICK #3: HOWEVER

"However" may be the most commonly abused adverb in student writing. Most students, however, do not know how to use it. Look at that last sentence. I used "however" correctly because I placed it in the middle of the sentence, with commas before and after. Do not place "however" (or any other adverb, for that matter) at the beginning of a sentence. People may tell you that nothing is grammatically wrong with a sentence such as this:

`However, they are not correct.`

But there is something wrong. Look at the comma. The reader must pause immediately after the first word in the sentence. This does not help your writing flow. Many sentences written in this manner will frustrate and bore the reader. Placing "however" at the end of a sentence is no better. If you must write "however," move it to the middle of the sentence. Your professor will thank you.

STYLE TRICK #4: FORMALITY

Do not address the reader with the word "you" in an academic essay. This usage wrongly assumes familiarity with your audience, and is too informal.

Incorrect:
`The tone of this poem makes you think of a`
`calm, peaceful place.`

Correct:
`This poem's language expresses peace and calm.`

Slang usages are also not acceptable in academic essays. Four-letter words and quirky, faddish expressions are also not allowed. Obscenities are never allowed, unless

52

they appear in a textual quotation from another source. Always choose better, more specific language, as in the following example:

Incorrect:
```
The antagonist in the story is a bitchy
stepmother.
```

Correct:
```
The story's antagonist is a cruel, manipulative
stepmother.
```

You may have noticed that throughout this book I have used the informal "you," passive constructions, and slang expressions. All of these things are forbidden in academic essays, which are formal and strict in their structure. This book is not an academic essay, however, and I am under no such constraints. I hope this book has taught you that academic writing has its own special rules, some of which do not apply anywhere else in the literary world. But freewriting, word choices, specific language, and awareness of audience are skills that can serve any writer.

Final Draft Format

I believe the best way to teach term paper format is through example. Instead of presenting a long list of rules, I have instead included a completed sample draft and a brief list. Simply observe the sample document for questions on spacing, punctuation, paragraph breaks, quotation, and the like.

The following list is by no means comprehensive. It does represent some simple answers to frequently asked questions. For more extensive grammar, punctuation, and format instruction, see the books listed in the BIBLIOG-RAPHY on page 62.

SPACING

Double space the entire paper vertically, including block quotations.

MARGINS

A one-inch margin surrounding the text is standard.

NOTES

If you are using only one classroom text for your paper, or you have only one resource, simple parenthetical notes are required. Parenthetical notes are simply page numbers or line numbers that appear in parentheses after your quotations. Notice that the notation is part of your sentence, and comes inside your sentence's period, but after the quotation marks. See the following examples.

For quoting prose, cite the page number:

```
". . . there is always a solution" (127).
```

For quoting poetry, cite the line number:

```
". . . and now my spinning is all done" (15).
```

For quoting drama, cite the act, scene, and line number, separated by periods:

```
". . . by the progress of the stars" (3.2.3).
```

If you are quoting from multiple sources, you will have to footnote your sources. For proper footnoting format, refer to your professor's guidelines, or the books in the BIBLIOGRAPHY, page 62.

TITLES

Underline titles of books, plays, films, magazines, newspapers, and book-length poems. Put quotation marks around the titles of shorter poems, magazine articles, short stories, and essays.

SINGLE QUOTATION MARKS

Single quotation marks are used when a quotation is embedded inside another quotation. Notice the triple quotation marks at the end of the sentence:

```
Uncle Sven used to say : "My father told me,
'Son, you are a fool.' "
```

SEMICOLON

Only use a semicolon if it separates two complete and related sentences:

```
The president is powerful; many people envy
this political position.
```

ELLIPSIS

If you wish to ignore words in a quotation, you may use an ellipsis in their place. An ellipsis is a series of three periods. Use ellipsis as follows:

```
"I shall return . . . and you shall repent"
(125).
```

COLON

A colon essentially alerts the reader to what follows. Use it to introduce a list, a block quotation, or a quotation that is a complete sentence unto itself. Always remember to put two spaces after:

```
John brought the food: bread, cheese, and a
bottle of wine.

Jill wonders aloud: "What am I doing here?"
```

Sample Paper

ASSIGNMENT

> In Franz Kafka's *Metamorphosis*, Gregor Samsa changes from a man into an insect. Examine the effects of this transformation on the members of his family. What is their reaction to this shocking occurrence? Can the story's title refer to something other than Gregor? Paper must be 4 to 5 pages in length.

SAMPLE INSTANT THESIS

> Although <u>the story is about Gregor turning into an insect</u>,
>
> Nevertheless <u>Grete's metamorphosis is the story's true focus</u>.
>
> Because <u>she begins the story as a childish teenager, she learns responsibility and gains confidence, and she eventually takes control of the family situation</u>.

SAMPLE FINAL DRAFT

The sample final draft begins below. Most papers do not require a cover page. Simply print your name, your professor's name, the class, and the date in the upper left corner. Center your title above the first paragraph as shown, and continue to follow the format as shown.

Jane Doe

Professor Smith

English 101

June 5, 1999

Sibling Transformation in Kafka's Metamorphosis

Franz Kafka's Metamorphosis opens with the
sentence: "When Gregor Samsa woke up one
morning from unsettling dreams, he found
himself changed in his bed into a monstrous
vermin" (3). This graphic and disturbing
transformation seems at first glance to be the
story's main focus. If we look further,
however, the title may refer to a different
mutation. Gregor's transformation causes his
sister, Grete, to change as well. As the story
progresses, Grete stops being a child and
gradually becomes a mature young woman.

When we first encounter Grete at the story's
beginning, she appears to be fragile and
helpless. Her family in the past has been
"annoyed with her because she had struck them
as being a little useless" (31). This all
changes once Gregor becomes an insect. Grete is
the only member of the family concerned about
Gregor's needs. Her compassion separates her

from her selfish mother and father when she
whispers through the door, "Gregor? Is
something the matter with you? Do you want
anything?" (6). Because Grete shows this
potential for caring, the stage is set for her
growth.

Even though Grete shows compassion for
Gregor, she is still a child inside. When
Gregor's manager comes to the apartment to
search for Gregor, Grete begins to cry. Her
reaction bothers Gregor, who wonders "what was
she crying about?" (11). Grete's childish
responses to a family crisis shows her
immaturity, but her compassion shows her
potential for growth.

Grete's growth and transformation begins
almost immediately following Gregor's change.
She begins to take control of situations and
events surrounding Gregor. For example, after
she hears Gregor's new "insect" voice, Grete
gives orders to her mother: "Go to the doctor's
immediately. Gregor is sick. Hurry, get the
doctor. Did you just hear Gregor talking?" (13).
Grete quickly becomes an authority in Gregor's
affairs, even more than his own parents are.

Grete's new confidence surrounding Gregor's
care spreads to all areas. She begins to help
her mother with the cooking, and takes

responsibility for Gregor's well-being. Gregor
is nearly starving after his transformation,
and Grete comes to the rescue. She not only
feeds Gregor, but attempts to discover what he
likes best. Grete brings him a "wide assortment
of things, all spread out on an old newspaper:
old, half-rotten vegetables; bones left over
from the evening meal . . . butter and salt"
(24).

Grete not only feeds Gregor, but mediates
between him and the rest of the family. When
her parents want to know anything about Gregor,
they must go through her first. She begins "to
adopt with her parents the role of the
particularly well-qualified expert whenever
Gregor's affairs were being discussed" (34).

Gregor himself resists the notion that his
sister is growing up, even though she now
controls his environment. Grete decides to move
Gregor's furniture from his room and enlists
help from her mother. Gregor watches through
his insect eyes from beneath the sofa, but
still does not acknowledge Grete's new
authority. He comments that her new-found
confidence and dedication comes from the
"romantic enthusiasm of girls her age" (34).
Gregor does not realize that he is under her
control completely. If it were not for Grete's

care he would die as a helpless insect.

Grete's new confidence gained at home transfers to the outside world as well. She begins to help support the family financially when she takes a job as a salesperson and begins to learn "shorthand and French in the evenings in order to attain a better position some time in the future" (41). Grete enters the adult world that Gregor left through his metamorphosis, and in doing so gains economic power with her confidence and maturity.

This new confidence, maturity, and power allows Grete to take action in any situation. Unfortunately for Gregor, Grete now has power enough to eliminate him. Grete eventually takes control of the household situation and declares what her parents do not have the courage to say. Grete pounds her fist on the table and pronounces:

> My dear parents . . . things can't go on like this. Maybe you don't realize it, but I do. I won't pronounce the name of my brother in front of this monster, and so all I say is: we have to try to get rid of it. (51)

Grete no longer sees her brother, and just sees an insect. Because Grete is the only mediator between Gregor and the family, her word is law. If Grete thinks Gregor is dead, the rest of the family can only agree. Grete now has more authority than any other family member.

Gregor dies shortly after Grete strips him of his identity. When she removes any emotional attachment between Gregor and the family, Grete breaks the connection that is causing the family to suffer. Gregor, as if in response to Grete's words, simply withers away. Grete's control over her environment and her position of power in the family enables her to remove the family's biggest threat.

In Kafka's Metamorphosis, Grete begins as a girl who cries at the first sign of trouble. She gains confidence and power throughout the story, however, until she has the power to remove the family's biggest problem. Gregor's metamorphosis from man to insect is perhaps the most shocking change in the book, but Grete's is the most important. Perhaps the book's first line should read: "One year Grete Samsa gradually transformed from a girl to a young and beautiful woman."

BIBLIOGRAPHY

Barzun, Jacques. *Simple and Direct: A Rhetoric for Writers.* New York: Harper, 1984.

Cook, Claire Kehrwald. *Line by Line: How to Edit Your Own Writing.* Boston: Houghton Mifflin, 1985.

Fowler, Ramsey H. *The Little, Brown Handbook.* Boston: Little, Brown, 1986.

Garrett-Goodyear, Joan H., Elizabeth W. Harries, Douglas L. Patey, Margaret L. Shook. *Writing Papers: A Handbook for Students at Smith College.* Smith College, 1980.

Guth, Hans P. *Words and Ideas: A Handbook for College Writing.* Belmont: Wadsworth, 1980.

Hodges, John C., Winifred Bryan Horner, Suzanne Strobeck Webb, Robert Keith Miller. *Harbrace College Handbook,* 12th Ed. New York: Harcourt Brace, 1994.

Kafka, Franz. *The Metamorphosis,* tr. Stanley Corngold. New York: Bantam Books, 1972. (All quotes from *The Metamorphosis* in the sample paper refer to this edition.)

McPherson, Elizabeth and Gregory Cowan, *Plain English, Please: A Rhetoric.* New York: Random House, 1986.

Payne, Lucile Vaughan. *The Lively Art of Writing.* New York: Penguin Books, 1969.

Strunk, William, Jr. and E. B. White, *The Elements of Style.* New York: Macmillan, 1979.

STEVEN POSUSTA: I came up with the idea for this book while working as a composition tutor at UCLA. I graduated from there in 1993 with honors and a degree in English. I have an MA degree in English Lit. from the University of Colorado where I taught Freshman Composition, wrote lots of papers, and finished the manuscript that became this book. Colorado suits me, because I like to mountain bike in the summer and snowboard in the winter.

BANDANNA BOOKS COLLEGE TITLES

quantity	title	@	price
___	**PAINLESS PERFECT GRAMMAR.** Strumpf & Douglas. Covers the sticky points of grammar. 127pp.	$12.95	___
___	**BENIGNA MACHIAVELLI.** Charlotte Perkins Gilman. Novel—a girl takes control of her destiny. 179pp.	$10.00	___
___	**ITALIAN FOR OPERA LOVERS.** ed. Hassan W. Ebron. Italian opera term		
___	**SURFING: A R** Surfing at its ori		
___	**SAPPHO: THE** tr. Sasha Newbo		
___	**ORIGINAL 18!** ed. A.S. Ash. 11		
___	**A BACKWARI** Walt Whitman.		
___	**AREOPAGITI(** ed. A.S. Ash. Ce		
___	**THE APOLOG** Socrates' classic		
___	**DANTE & HIS** Italian love sonn		
___	**GHAZALS OF** arguing with Go		
___	**THE LITTLE G** translation of the		
___	**GANDHI ON** Bhagavad Gita		

Orde

Visit (
Credi

*Teacher supplemen